In my mind Thoughts

I0420342

Laura Johnson

DEDICATION

To all of you, dear readers.

CONTENTS

CHAPTER 1

I saw the sky, its bricks falling down, the false sky or roof they built to disguise the truth hidden from us, for a long time, making us think false, the things and all what we see are not what they seem to be, are not what they are, they hide the number of spiritual people in this world, all are converting to be or should I say all are already spiritual believers, only few are not, and those few controlling the world blinded us for so long.

I tapped the shoulder of Mike saying: "look, the sky is falling and the truth is here", suddenly the floors made of concrete cracked, the few left, the "non spiritual" panicked and are trying to build back the false sky to hide the truth from people.

He "the man" holds a board, he is talking to a woman they are trying to make a new plan in there bizarre space kind of outfits.

Tyra was sitting on the floor, I was afraid that she gets hurt, so I told her to stay by the circular stair while I go talk to "the man", they don't want us to know what's going on, but I already know, I put my feet on the broken concrete floor carefully, it still holds me, I can get to the other side where that man is in a kind of space room,

I see button lights everywhere.

Behind me are the people I care for. Suddenly, I see this girl from my old house's window, the house is the one I lived in when I was twelve years old, she is talking and laughing happy being young ... I don't care if she tries to intimidate me because she is young and I'm not, I'm not the type to be intimidated by the "youth and softer skin".

Being young is just an outside soft skin but I don't want to go back to the past except to be with him again him my father.

He who loved me, loved us and all the universe! He who respected everyone and much more the kids, the future, our future builders as he called them.

I went to brush my hair and do the braids as usual feeling sleepy, lazy and feverish.

I got up because I love to do so...it's a new day!.

I want the future generation to be better than us!.

Life is tough we need to toughen up and adjust our skin to the environment.

they complain about air poisoning and pollution harming the trees and... What about us the same Kind? Why don't we look at each other anymore, why we... Us hate each other, losing the confidence I used to have after going through difficult times...

I' m trying to bring me back, I used to understand the surrounding by stating all my thoughts to express me, myself.

I couldn't understand why the guy hits the girl? why the girl hurts the girl? The mess we are in right now, where to go from here no idea!.

Fights and argues are daily scenarios in my life, I want to be happy, I want to have a normal life, as a reaction I yell then again hurt the ears of the people around me, I reply harshly to their anger, they are just...

Putting them under stress is not good, I know it isn't, but, I keep doing the same wrong thing everyday, they mentioned: "Everyday, you do that to us, every single day...".

A hug calms me, deep I'm sad to make them sad, deep I'm sorry to them and to myself for being such a monster, unbearable to live with and have around.

My childhood was happy, I come from a stable family, so why am I doing that to them?

Today, this morning my same habit, enjoy the coffee with black and white cookies, watch the TV, nothing interesting in my opinion they are wasting my time, so instead I got up to finish the work I started a week ago, got bitten by obstacles and silly things out of my hand which stopped me to finish, but also got used to being lazy and not wanting to do it, this is not good...

So, here I was, very bizarre, I told Mike to look at the ships flying in the space, above us, they are coming, but will disappear quick, I had to tell him to witness seeing them, they are up there, they are here already! it's like having a proof of what me and my girlfriend Zoe saw once, it was just the two of us, two triangular shaped vessels disappeared in a fraction of a second, they were so fast moving, it's not human's ships for sure those are ahead of us or smarter in a technology term, Zoe mentioned to me that she will not witness that event to anyone and if I spoke about it she will deny it if I bring her name...This time I wanted Mike to witness.

Now, I recall a man who was half shaved, they? They were injecting him with a liquid, I understood that it was a rule, an obligation to go through, the future seemed dark to me, that injection is to control human kind, it had to be in the apparent nerve of the neck from behind, the weird thing is that it looked just like the blood of another human! He did take it, but, in my mind is he a good man? whatever he is with the darkness around him I couldn't see properly, so I just saw the hands injecting the needle of a long thin syringe, he was sitting.

I still want to go talk to the somewhat guy "the man" in the that weird suit, the whole scene is in two colors, grey and white except for the syringe that did hold

the blood, Red color liquid, the suit was dark grey but I remember the triangular shape, from the neck to the abdomen a V down shape, darker than grey a little.

What are they planning to do again? Hide the truth from us the truth is out there, the sky broke down didn't it?

the ships that were hidden now I see them again, it's true, they are out there in the space.

That girl happy being young, I didn't care about her.

Now I have to get a cab, I'm not young anymore but to myself I'm beautiful.

Are the people going to be friendly to me ?

I'm not attracting the attention I used to, someone might say I'm crazy not to just enjoyed that time, I wasn't and couldn't, it brought me many problems being in the wrong place and surrounded by the wrong people.

Let's get back to were I was...I wanted to take a cab, it shouldn't be difficult I'm not young anymore so what?

I really don't care, but, the people I didn't meet for a while will they think I'm not the same or that I'm crippled? that's what they use for being old.

Should that matters to me? or is it just because I have been thinking to go back to the old place?.

The changes, I hate the changes when I wasn't part of them... Haaaa.

Don't be fooled by me I care less haaaa...

Funny ha! I remembered, I was with my dad that day walking, and suddenly, out of the blue started to laugh like a real crazy person, I was happy but didn't have any conversation with my dad, I just remembered a funny incident that happened to me, I cannot recall exactly but it was funny, my dad asked, what's the reason and what's so hilarious to laugh in that crazy way in the street? I remember answering, silence makes me laugh it's so funny dad, I always laugh when it is silent as if someone is tickling me hard.

What am I going to do today mmmm... no idea, I love to live my life taking it easy and day by day.

For quite sometime now, I haven't been myself, I mean good, between the swearing and the swearing, being nasty was the brand I stamped myself with.

I couldn't understand that what happened in my life or to me did for a reason.

Nancy opened my eyes months ago, therefore I came back to my faith again, I know I trust Him, I know He is here, without Him I cannot find a meaning to live such a life, everyday has been a challenge for me.

You know over the years I got down from the loss in and out, the money I still think is not everything, yes we need it but we shouldn't stress over it, the little is good enough, why I'm not happy? why my life is not what I pictured? is being a true person wrong?.

I'm surrounded by fake faces and people they pretend to be my friends, who they think themselves fooling? I'm too stupid!.

Naive is seen as a weakness, they interpreted it as stupid, this is not what I am, I knew when I was taking advantage of, but yes certainly I was duped to believe in friendship and the people giving their word as a binding promise to not mess up with my staff did and were in fact acting, they still act but I don't care and I pretend like nothing happened.

It's OK, money for me is nothing, well maybe something these months since... The big short story is that there is so much to tell about this surrounding and how badly it affect each one of us, that I feel I need to go, just go to another planet and live with aliens! They might have heart to love one another with respect and peace!.

Travel far enough to never be around that's my story for today, I'm thinking to cook some pasta or pizza then just take it easy for the rest of the afternoon.

I want to tell you that I'm thinking strongly about eating which disturbs my thoughts.

Things sometimes take years if not a whole

life to be finished for reasons, obscure and not ordinary, hard to explain but I'll share with you that creature, a mysterious yet true creature that harmed me just by looking at me, I was in a depression phase!.

Is it because I missed my father or because the people harmed me so much?.

I know, I lost it in that time but I also know I had a condition...

CHAPTER 2

Yesterday, it was the second time that I saw a co-worker, the first time was seeing him talking to someone, in my mind, he is back, and not working anymore with the client's side, who didn't have much work, so he decided to go back to the previous company where his ally is there to babysit him and give him a hand again as it's the habit of this guy to do so for his fellows.

I don't like that guy he is a monster hiding behind that mask, he is lazy, he takes the credits for doing nothing and makes others take the blames for his mistakes behind their backs of course, it's like he and his ally own the company, What about the real owner? does he know about the corruption and the under table deals?.

But why was I bothered by someone like him?.

Again, in my mind, I had an interview about what I can do at work and what am I good at doing?.

I kept repeating the same words, there were two guys doing the interview.

Am I going to work with this type? Again! Hell no, I don't want it.

Over the years many people suffering, were treated like if they were nothing.

What's happening? Do we need nasty people? hell no, we don't!.

I might sound angry but... it's just seeing that bad guy and hearing his name twice in a row bothers me.

This girl, comes and takes some rare tea each time from my box, I didn't mind, again and again, not much left in my cute rare box, I, we are like in a dormant, at the university, she comes... I hear my grandma Saying to that girl "NO, you won't have any more go get yours, that's it with you, I will not allow you finishing the tea of my grand kid", and with a knife in my hand I'm cleaning the rust from that box, it's becoming shinier and cleaner, I love it! I checked on the tea, not much left and it's so rare to get, my grandma is right, I didn't say a word and that girl understood not to ask for it ever again.

My friend Tyra's magazine in my hand, I handed it to the girl of the dormant and tea.

I see a two sided door, on it it says "neighbor", I went through it, did the interview with the two guys, I heard the name of the mean guy, but previously my girlfriend's face appeared and her voice saying: "I spoke to him he is looking for someone to hire", in my thoughts and mind... He is looking for a donkey to do his work and slave while he socializes with wealthy and high ranked bosses.

I finished my interview with that guy, I

don't know who he is? He has a mustache that's all what I really remember.

I went in a hurry to that girl, she had a short straight dark hair, I don't care about her, I grabbed the magazine, Tyra's one!

she asked: "is she going to ..." I decided not to answer her, I don't know her, she is too audacious to ask such question, she is in my opinion too curious, so I had to stop her right there.

I turned my face, pushed the two sided door, held Tyra then went trough the stairs, was it down? I don't like it if it's down, I want it to be upstairs, but where are we heading taught? no clue! I heard a loud scream, saying she "Tyra" is in pain from the cold drink, I checked the time then asked her to come under the blanket to keep warm and for the pain to disappear, she believed me, and so she did.

last time, I heard my girlfriend Rachel singing, her voice was so beautiful! oh how much I miss her yet feel I'm a stranger, almost 15 years didn't see her, it was just talking over the phone, she always no matter what makes sure I'm laughing and happy, while she, her life is not so great, I love the way she turns things from sad to laugh, to whatever who cares after all.

We all go through rough time not that way taught but let's talk about something else instead, right now!.

I had my coffee that I enjoy by cheating and adding some milk to it, I cannot handle anymore the pure black one, had many cookies that I was advised not to touch anymore, why am I doing that to me? I know it's bad for sake, didn't I learn from what happened to me not far ago... two months ago, didn't I come back to life? Thanks to God, from who I asked forgiveness for my bad and angry behavior.

I thank God for helping me get out before my boat sinks, before I dive to the darkness without return.

What are my plans for today? Mmmm let's see, with my busy schedules haaaa fooling around... I called my friend Tessa for her birthday, I hope she is fine, didn't get hold of her but instead got hold of someone? Anyway, didn't get to hear her voice for months now, I feel I'm the bad seed that cut off with the roots, in reality I miss my friends, but long distance, no phone cards, no Skype, it is difficult to keep in touch, I just keep asking my friend Kelly who calls me often how they are doing, and of course the answer is that they are just fine, take it easy and don't worry.

I saw Rachel, my dear friend on a bicycle, lying down on her tummy, her bums naked, her hands holding the handles of the bicycle, I wonder what's going on?

why is she in this position giving the chance to the white polar bold bear to bite her, eat her and therefore kill her!.

I was disturbed by this, but, what can I do? pretend as I have been told to not pay attention and just ignore it? The polar bold bear had sharp teeth, he started to grab her and deepen his teeth in her left bum, I tapped his shoulder trying to discourage him to do so without letting him know of my intention, I pretended to have a conversation with him, I don't like him and certainly I don't trust him, in my mind go get him some meat to get him away from my friend, in my mind I don't think I have enough food to bribe him, in my mind I cannot go to the fridge, if I'm not around, in a second he can swallow her after cutting her with its long tooth, I'm weak, I'm scared, I'm trying but he didn't care for me and got his teeth too deep that I cannot help it, she is in a huge pain but handling it, it hurts, I feel her pains, I'm hurt, I don't want her harmed, she is not screaming I'm terrified!

She needs help NOW, I'm breathing fast from what I saw, I knew she is in trouble, but I knew she told the awful bold bear everything about her situation, and his plan was to harm her and get her down, why is she so naive? Why did she tell him? didn't she learn from her past to not be naive, we live in a world of savage animals in a form of human body, if she is a bird at least don't get near the snake or don't tell it your weak situation!

Scary part two when I was searching something, my friend Kelly called, she mentioned how worried she is regarding Rachel! Now I'm scared, I listened to her mentioning that there is a guy untrustworthy, a devil to avoid, he is trying to harm Rachel, she even gave me that he is an old guy! wow the bold curved polar bear untrustworthy, without stopping her, she mentioned that she screamed terrified from his malicious thoughts to harm our friend, my story that matches hers.

Rachel is in danger, I mentioned to her to watch out, to not get hurt, she opened up to me about the truth.

She found a job and had to work for cents with the bold old bear, the crippled nasty man!.

CHAPTER 3

I'm taking a bath, I'm wearing my cloths now, the old women is talking to me stating how much great work she and the other girl, both did with that guy.

The walls are in a purple color because of the plants in rows hard to recall the name of that flower's type, but well garnished well organized.

I mentioned to her how beautiful it is and

asked if I may join to finish the project, in my mind she doesn't want me to do so, I noticed she wasn't qualified, good for her I didn't mind.

She is hard to deal with, but yet she is refusing to let me in, in my mind, it's good to earn some money doing easy and simple things I had experience with, no way, she is making excuses and trying to block me from getting what I want, I deserve it because I'm more skilled than she is.

In my mind that old woman is not nice, not a friend as she pretends to be.

I was busy watching Korean movies, I just discovered Daniel Henney, oh my!.

Loved the movie "Seducing Mr.perfect", of course the chemistry was amazing, it makes you believe in beauty and love.

I saw Dave coming few steps downstairs with me to the entrance of the old building I used to live in, it's not the one of my apartment, he went ahead after this restaurant and chose two others without telling me, he discovered them, while walking with me, why is he keeping it a secret? Why he always lives another life? He is a dark person, I don't think he is my friend as he always shocks me with cruel acts.

In the appearance he is nice... He is an actor.

How can he live two lives, have two faces?

I'm worried about him thought! I see him tired, I don't like his face, he looks exhausted and needs rest, mmmm... He was talking to Nancy and in my mind I'm like... He is tired and needs help! Under his eyes, a purple colored part and one eye is higher than the other, his face makes me worried! Well from outside the box he does everything, I shouldn't complain, he is kind but I don't like the way he reacts to my talking and feel he is fake, it's too obvious, I don't care who he is because I don't like that person, period!.

He just called to ask what I need?.

Let's move on to my boring day, after my shower, I cooked the chicken soup and cleaned slightly the toilets, I cannot push too hard and clean well yet, it takes time to heal.

Strange, I don't recall the details of the tea girl part but, I'm talking to that blond I've never seen before, Ethan gave her a pair of transparent earrings, I've told her that they are gorgeous, in fact I've had a pair better than hers, I wanted just to be nice to her specially that I worked with Ethan before, I asked him to give me his ring, I wanted it so badly that I gave him mine, I knew it's good to get and own his, but he puts down mine and refused to give me his, so I asked him to return mine that I saw laying on the hard floor by his side and wore it back.

I was still happy, he gave me much more jewelry and rings, all in gold and even a bracelet! Saying: "here it is you can take all that, I'm giving it to you", my hand was full of gold, of jewelry, I went back to the office, which wasn't mine, it's were the two previous women I wanted to help work, the windows were open and I felt the breeze coming from them, I loved it, in my mind why always these two complain?.

This is really nice, they took me there to see were they work.

We Don't like it much, they mentioned, it should've been a better condition they continued... Better than that!

I'm in a rocking chair, talking to the older women, she asked: "you still want to work here?" I answered by moving my head in a "no" direction, I don't want to do it anymore, she understood that, I wanted to do something else instead, I don't know what yet thought!

I'm standing and walking in the office that looks like a comfortable house and of course the nasty girl saw what it's in my hand, she wanted to take it, as usual and always she wants what I have.

I bought earlier a piece of dough to make bread but this guy, a manager, sold me a huge piece, in the beginning I said: "too much for me" but then he insisted and I didn't mind, I took it.

One guy pretending to be my friend had to cook it in the microwave, it did make four portions of a traditional home bread, but he had to let them cook in the microwave, one portion at the time, it's huge, he burned them though, and not only that he gave them to other people, they are eating them at the round high table, why did he do that, he is a guy I knew, he in the past did hit me in the back.

When I discovered his real face I stopped the friendship, and he continued to harm me, he still harms me?!.

I got the dough from that manager, he is at the large yellow round table with another guy, I see this girl with the black hair wearing a nice red barrette, a flat thin one, she passes by, Corine asked me what I think about her, she is gorgeous I mentioned and wearing her hair very nicely, I understood Corine is jealous of her, the manager likes that girl very much, I can understand why! ha...

But before all that, I was in a tunnel, I'm coming out of the place with its unique rocky mountains and tunnels, I can see now from the road the cars parked down there, that girl I met her already before! Was she really a nice person? not as far as I remember, in my mind, no ....

Yesterday, I was watching the Korean

movie again, I cannot have enough of "Seducing Mr. perfect" what a beautiful romance and chemistry between the two!

it relaxes me, that movie makes me believe that there is still love out there, I used to think so until things in my life got rough, nasty and stressful, I met the wrong people, all of them did hurt me and still do, why? No clue! But all what I know is that this world is rough for the nice ones.

CHAPTER 4

I see Selena, coming nearby and smiling at me, I didn't bother saying hi to her, basically it's like OK she is here and me too, but while she was leaving I started to follow her, I wanted to ask her an autograph, I forgot, Tyra loves her, and bringing an autograph for her from her favorite person would be amazing!.

I called Selena, that place got crowded somehow, so I tried to tap on her back and shoulder, no way, I was close but missed, she didn't turn to me, I was close but couldn't touch her to let her know I'm behind, still, I insisted and followed her to wherever she is going, shortly she sat on her amazing chair, in her right side a girl seating, but in a darker spot, I couldn't know and see who she was, I smiled to Selena she turned to me in an upset way, she didn't look happy to see me, why?

In my mind, it's all because when I got a chance to get to talk to her and smile back, I didn't, so now that I'm willing to do so she is not! It's like I missed my opportunity.

It's the Egyptian time and that guy with that scarf on the head similar to

Cleopatra's time, has a Bible on the table!

I looked at the book, in my mind why is he having a Bible? as far as I know it wasn't the religion of pharaoh! in my mind, I saw a second ago someone holding the Quran, but it's not in his hands anymore? where is it?.

Me and my friend Dave are trying to choose the madeleines that I made, picking the ones that look and taste good, we have a pile of them, I remember

Saying: "oh, I did a good job" while biting each time the little ones and trying to leave the bigger, better looking to be used and showed later on, that girl was sitting and watching us, that girl is a witch, very mean, she took advantage and in an unbelievable speed got a piece from the pile, her arm got so long and fast, in my mind, oh no! this is not good.

I'm not too excited today, what happened was worse than the previous events, I see my friend Nancy, and hear her saying: "that girl, who I see only her head's picture is getting a baby soon", she adds: "that's good", the girls in the picture at a high speed run to do the intervention to get pregnant, I really wish her the best.

Nancy, continued saying: "you know after the pain happiness might come, from which I understood that while I have pain, somebody else might be happy.

I see Oscar walking with that bad women, who looks like my nasty cousin, while she is telling me the type of women Oscar is cheating with or will cheat with, she is forcing, pulling out his ring, he didn't stop her, but instead allowed her to do so even if the ring was like almost glued to his finger, his face is weird, and reflects the ugliness of his act.

I'm turning to talk to Nancy, "see" I said, "I think it's over with his girlfriend after cheating on her", Nancy confirmed and added: "a lot of good and happy moments I wish for Zoe, what counts, is seeing her happy sometimes!.

Wow, the girl in my cousin's appearance is very bad, she brings pain.

My cousin stole a man, let's say a cheater man, from a wonderful lady who had a daughter that I met once walking on the beach with Nancy, I knew then what she's done to this lady, steeling her husband, the father of a very adorable beautiful girl, I saw tears in her eyes mentioning my awful cousin and what she had done to her stable home that used to be once.

My cousin the witch got a son soon after her secret wedding with that insane old crocked man, nobody would've married her, but foolish he did indeed and got a son with her if he is the real father as she continues to flirt and sleep with younger guys.

That witch is coming with Oscar to destroy the joy.

Dave used to be my friend, being honest, he is not as nice as he seems or as I mentioned to others, he has this awful side that he used to complain about... His dad's character, yes it was wrong to go against the principles, I taught he was OK, a real joke, he faked it, he mentioned one day that he is liberal, wow how much he changed!.

I, again, had today a big headache, it's probably the season, I'm sneezing, tears in the eyes, I hope I don't catch the virus, especially that we live in a world full of pollution.

What's wrong with those advertisers, always and many times in a row calling, it bothers me, if I pick they get glued to me talking about their products and promotions, I don't want to be rude to them, that's why I prefer not to pick it, but it's annoying.

Sometimes, they call late in the night,

other times in the weekend so damn early, you can imagine someone needing rest and when that phone rings, you could actually hear it from very far, so loud and no volume control to minimize its sound!

I see my previous supervisor having kindness towards helping me with the reference, he is with the girl that he cares for and likes so much, he listened to her, she wants him to help me, we were on the balcony of a high building.

I look through the balcony's glass door, the classroom is full of students, I'm wondering if I should get in, it's jut like a sneak peek, earlier-on, a second ago I was in the bathroom trying for a pee, I couldn't do it, this person, a girl is annoying me, I cannot do it in front of her plus the poop is everywhere on the toilets, none is clean, I took of my underwear, tried, then decided to do it later when there is a little privacy, this toilet has no door anyway.

CHAPTER 5

I see the shore but cannot reach it why? me and him 'Daniel' didn't know how to paddle the little boat, I took Abby, put her between my legs, then get to hold her tight, the floating boat is up and down the thick ocean's waves, we didn't and couldn't manage to stabilize the boat and navigate to the shore, in my mind, Daniel is slowing us, the little boat looses it's balance because of him, in my mind, he should jump in the ocean while pushing us, then manage to swim and bring himself to the shore.

I see a crowd over there "the shore" looking at us, he is trying to sit on the back end, it's a little better but not much, still struggling, still hard to make it, I don't want to loose control and flip into the deep ocean,

in my mind, I cannot suggest that he jumps and swims, we cannot see what's underneath us, it could be really dangerous, to face the unknown.

We should stick together no matter what, but he is delaying us, delaying me, I started to navigate using my hands which opened like paddlers we finally started to move slowly but surely.

I hear her, Sofia, I see her face, telling her dad he should get me the elegant

chair similar to hers, a copy, on it its written 2011, it seems that this number reflects the best chair.

I hear her asking him to get me the best location, the best of this and that, similar to what he got for her, she just got a good job, a new location after working for a long time in a very poisonous place.

I look at the wall, with all the instructions being given to her dad who holds a good position and works for a governmental company.

I met this author, he was wearing glasses, young, with a blond and wetted hair, he signed the book of an unknown guy even though he wasn't asked to do so.

I took the opportunity and asked for a signature as well, he refused! Why? it looks like he doesn't like me, who is he anyway? What is he thinking of himself?.

I was disappointed in him, I don't see him anymore as an idle, I don't need his signature, if he is that awful!

I'm in a car, going very fast, I'm with Mel, everything is brown color, the bridge, the walls, it's so fast, it's so scary, I don't want to hit those walls.

We passed the bridge came to a turn, oh, no! In my mind, we will crush! At my surprise, we made the turn, we are safe for now, but he shouldn't be driving this way, like a fool and crazy, I better get off and save my skin, I don't like that craziness and speeding at all, is he trying to harm me? Who is this mean person?.

I see Tessa and Rachel peeing, then they crossed the road safely, Rachel wetted her clothes and my hands too, I helped her dry herself with a piece of fabric that I set aside to clean it later on.

The Path, I was there, I see Rachel talking to that girl, is she? She is telling her to take the job opportunity seriously and to work harder, it looks like a school but...

I took Tyra aside to the other shaded place with less traffic, in my hand a pot of soup to feed her some, she needs to eat something, that side was a little narrow, what if the traffic starts, after we moved there away from the crowd to have some peace and be tranquil? In my mind, people can squeeze in and pass by, we have good space and distance to be still fine to pass by and make it through.

That branch, full of leaves, too close to the sidewalk were we are, I made sure not to be bothered by it, it brings shade if the sun gets stronger, and gives us privacy to not be bothered by anyone.

Other than that I made some pancake for breakfast, I love having them with the syrup in the weekend, it's becoming a hobby, a habit, every weekend I have to make it.

I'm climbing stairs, few only, I have a place

to go to, I see three unique stones among many, standing out, they look like dominoes with red, yellow, and blue lines on them, they are so different than the rest which are very plain and are plenty of them everywhere.

There is this boy, with a blond hair, crying and screaming to get the special dominoes, I see and hear his father saying that it's not his, therefore, he cannot have them.

The three unique stones are in my hand, I'm taking them to Tyra, but in the middle of the hall, his father was shocked when I gave him all of them, I gave him the beautiful and priceless stones, that tapped his head, what a funny sound it made, I said to myself, his son is not nice, he didn't bother to catch the stones and let them fall on the ground, he who had tons of stones but none like these three ones I gave him.

I was called the next day, my friend cannot make the 3 o'clock appointment and Tyra will not be able to meet Austin.

Tyra likes him, found him very nice, and considers him a good friend, she talks about him a lot!

I'm attached to a cord by the feet, falling deep in the empty dark patio of a gigantic building, was saved by the cord, I managed very well no problem, but falling is frightening.

I have these small cute plastic wings, I stand in the air, Rachel came to talk to me, I'm up in the hall talking to her, in front of me a dormitory room door, I see light, like morning, that room is so bright that I couldn't see what's inside it.

I see a penny, a copper one on the hall's ground, I didn't pick it, it's not mine, why is it there on my way?

I'm in the old hunted apartment, yes our old apartment is possessed by a very dangerous creature, grandma told me that she "the spirit woman" visited her few times, grandma can see the others, the parallel living in our world.

I'm there sitting, my friend Zoe came, sat, and asked me if I had something to tell her, she is trying to know details, who was she really? in the form of my friend Zoe!, a mean ugly witch, trying to get details of my daily life! In my mind, I know, that apartment is hunted...

CHAPTER 6

I'm jumping on roofs, from one to another, it's night time, I'm holding a pair of black colored pants, which are damaged and cut in the back, Ray is talking to me, I'm explaining to him that the guy who is working there and knows him is not to be trusted, in my mind he is there to do him some harm, but, I continued and said that the front pants still look fine and that who cares about the back, just to reassure him that I'm there to help and that he has just to have faith and continue working for that unethical company, which never deserves a hard working person, as all the people they care for are unethical man and women, pretending to be kind in their outside, but are black devil hearted people, putting masks on their sweet poisonous faces.

It's all about who you drink and socialize with of course, cheating you is their rule to be...

I see her, Nancy, hugging tight and holding to her chest a baby, a problem that she is carrying in her life.

She suffered and still in her old age, God helps this mother, who suffered and still suffers, no ending, no limits to her suffering...

In my mind, yes, she made it and she carries a huge sad worry, still she made it to the house where it might be better or worse we really don't know.

It's a burden to take care of such problem but faith just faith, forever no matter what.

I'm called on the phone, thank God, Nancy, she and her girlfriends aren't there anymore, what a relief, even though it's not the best, what can you do...!.

He, Austin came, I see bandages all over, I'm asking him what's going on? I didn't bother even to say bye or see you to him yesterday, I'm always a real nasty person in all the ugly way, meaning yelling screaming, that's what I do when he doesn't listen, and he never does or will do, I should stop it's not healthy for me, nor for him, my close surrounding is suffering, it's like I want them to hate me, whatsoever?.

I'm asking him, he doesn't reply as usual, it wasn't nothing it was the worse, I started crying, screaming of pain, sadness and regret, I didn't treat him as a friend, I hated him every day to the worse, but he helped me to get to that point when he chocked me with all the ugly surprises, what can I say, he helped, and now I'm this way, nasty!

Me and Dave are with the woman, the doctor, in her office, she is cleaning, and I helped because she couldn't reach all of the hole, I did what I can, but, in my mind, still some to do, deeper, she is bending herself to show her bum to him and get him interested, but the wooden desk is hiding half of her bottom's body because she is half in the desk, where I see the spider web on its side, no cleaning has been done for a long time, but I'm not going to touch or clean it should I? She didn't see that it needs undusting? She doesn't have a house keeper? We are on the couch both me and my friend Dave, she is standing, my friend wrote something secretly and gave it to her, he smiled, she laughed so loud, in my mind they are up to something and kept me stupid and disrespected, I decided to get out of her office, after all they are playing a dishonest game, I opened the door, it's grey and raining, I cannot go too far this way, I care about him but what am I supposed to do? I meet, on the street this girl that has eye liner makeup, she is married, she tells me that the women doctor is known for her misbehavior and scandalous acts, and that all the village and community know, she is always corrupting relationships, destroying families with the stupid guys easy to fall in her games because they want to, are irresponsible, and as well they are same trash type as her, I decided walking backward, she tries to hold me to avoid the embarrassment, she knew what's going to happen, she is trying, they know her trashy moves, I didn't listen and opened the door, she was naked, he was sitting on a sofa, with his pants down, ready for her to do it, he is taking it with a huge desire like he was just waiting for the minimum sign, I looked, he was ready, in my mind, he really wants the trashy to get him and use him as she wishes, I looked, she puts makeup on to make him like her, she is a real trash, same as he, from the same trashy type, from having the dark long dress down and being exposing herself naked to him to suddenly having a velvet dress well done hair and makeup...!.

I'm on the big bed, it's dark, I cannot see, I'm moving but I don't have an underwear, my private part was seen by a witch, an awful woman ho harmed me and still envy me, I've been told while I was swimming in the ocean, in my room, the parallel woman was swimming with me and saw me naked then told the witch details.

I'm sitting on the floor and Dave was in a car, not his, a woman, the same trashy one of earlier on comes to me and asked that I should get up and go with him, but I don't want to, I'm upset and lost believe in him and lost trust.

I have Tyra in between my knees, she pulls me from my elbow, she repeats: "you should go with them, him", she pulls insisting, I got up and went to join them in that car...

I saw my dad, what does he want, I don't recall, all what I do remember is him in front of me behind sets of things are they mine? He mentioned something what was it? It's important to recall but I don't!.

CHAPTER 7

I see Kim with her beautiful naked body, flying steady facing a huge tall fancy and royal window, she can be up in the air, she is beautiful, she looks at her left shoulder and kiss it, she has a royal bed... the woman watching her hired her to do a show.

Kim looked at the woman and made it clear that she demands respect otherwise she will disappear from the huge show, that woman should listen to Kim otherwise she looses her.

I remember something..., me and my father pushed the two sided door and went through it..., huge light!.

That unknown young guy held from his feet, up to the roof, at the university place, almost did fall, I wished him to do so, but the older man caught him on time, that must be his support, in my mind he is not knowledgeable and worthless yet he got to be there, he has a mustache, he is a guy of his word, is he...? Still, I don't like him, I want it to be me.

At the long table I'm watching the man and the woman, screaming shouting socializing, are they instructors? Some sort of an academic team? I see two short haired women, they are with them, I run downstairs, one of them is going the same direction, the other one is driving a black car, I hear the one closer to me stating that the other woman got to the position she is now holding thanks to a push, she clarifies to me that nothing comes with just hard work, it's who you know over what you know.

She wanted the position, I wished for too, it's clear now that the opportunity is given just to few, through using their friends and related ones, any relationships are used to get it, nothing in this world is innocent, the innocence is lost a long time ago! Or at least it feels like it!

That guy is in the classroom, all the girls like him, he is cute, suddenly he trows a two headed fork up in the air, then an explosion through it, one piece got his tummy, he took it out no problems and stood up after being bended backward! He runs out to be safe, I understood then that no chance for me to make it as he did, and that careers are given trough shoulders "Networking".

I'm in the bus, Abby is standing between my legs, I'm trying not to fall but there is not much to hold onto in this weird bus, where a bad man I see sitting is trying to harm someone, the bus has few kids, I understood that falling from the bus is easy.

I'm on the sidewalk of the road talking and explaining something to someone.

My Friends Zoe and Rachel are sitting in the living room, same as years ago as far as I remember we all sit to watch TV in that room, it seems that it is my place too, Austin is not showing any kindness, he is telling them what to do and what not, similar to a play on TV, too loud but they are not listening to him.

I followed Austin and mentioned to him that he should be nice to them, came Kelly? It's not really her it's the woman "doctor", she is trying with him again, she cried loud to him: "I don't have a ring!" he replied entering another room: "me neither" and I topped that: "me neither" she tried earlier to sit by his side but I pulled her away from him, because he deserves someone else.

He is my friend, but, found that him keeping secrets from me is a killer, he never expresses himself or...weird.

Abby creamed, her pains started, she is suffering, I couldn't even apply the gel on her so my friend Sam took care and held her up hoping for that pain to stop, I went away.

I had my cup of coffee with cookies, I will try to finish the movie I started yesterday.

But few people are around, one of them was my dear dad talking and showing things on that long table, in my mind, dead people sitting along that table, he is telling me something, what was it?

I'm sitting, being part of a show, why though? I see him? him Joe, I had a girlfriend, whenever someone asks me to be his, she tells me that he asked her out, she is a sick person, I didn't care, it took me many years to discover her lies, she flirts a lot with guys.

I used to tell her when a guy asks me out, and weird enough she asks me to point the guy in person to her, then, the next thing you know she tells me that he asked her out, guys, they are so silly, but now of course, I know and we all "her friends" do know she lies, anyway, Joe wanted to be with me and one day came in person to ask me to be his, I went to the room and told

Kelly about it, but she had an eye on him, Joe is known to be handsome, Kelly said to me: "impossible, you lie, he didn't ask you to be his".

Joe is from England, came to study and will go back when he finishes his engineering degree, we met at the beach, I didn't like him since he called me "Madam!", "rude from him" I told myself, but discovered that he said it by respect, I was 18 years old! I decided not to like him then, since I wasn't interested in guys, even though I knew that deep inside I really like him I walked away.

He was different in every way, stunning beauty and stunning kindness.

Kelly came to my room the next day telling me he is interested in her, I believed her, so when he stopped to say hi, I gave him my back to never again say back hi to him, ever again, after the years passed she opened up to me, telling me that he never did ask her out, but it's too late, life moved on!

Here is the thing, Kelly couldn't believe that Joe asked me out, he said it to few people, she screamed: "it's impossible, no way that he did, no way!".

Her jealousy started to be obvious, but I lost him already, because of a lie of a close dear jealous girlfriend.

Still, I love Kelly no matter what, and always will do, because to me she is more important, not the guys, even deep I know that he wasn't like others, he stood out! But, after all it's the past now.

So, I see Joe and hear him singing, he is playing guitar, behind him a white theater curtain, holding the microphone, Joe is sitting on a chair, I hear a voice saying: "you don't have a good voice", he turns to where the scream came from, smiled, then continued singing, in my mind, yes true, his voice is not that great to have a show, I was sitting with the public.

Now, I'm on a bench, me, my girlfriend Kelly and others, I think, I worked with few of them before, but, in my mind it's a game show, I'm there, I see my red hair down, and I'm wearing white, in my mind, I'm young! We all are waiting for Joe's show to start, on the left end side, I see the Jazz teacher, she asked me to put makeup on kids for the show, I said: "yes, but, I don't know how to do it?" She has some salads and other foods, she cooks a lot, apparently, I held her hand, went after to be with Abby, she didn't eat the whole day, it was a long waiting day for the show, she wears her suite, each kid has a changing room, similar to the one in stores, with a door you can lock, Abby needs to pie, but suddenly, I'm getting my long smooth poop out, so I held her to not sit on the toilet, full of different people's poops, she peed and got my legs wet, my hands too. We are back, where the teacher is, in the kitchen, one teenage girl tells me that she took care a little bit of Abby and gave her some bread, I thanked her for doing do.

Abby is sitting on the stairs, by a toilet's cabin, an old-fashioned style one, built from wood.

I got my cup of coffee as usual, feeling it is cold already, winter is here, hoping that I do something today! Hope it works, because every day is the same, I need to look for something that I enjoy doing, cooking, maybe? For a change!.

The truth is, in the Job's world, it is always difficult to get what you want, it takes time, skills and efforts, but some people without any experience, use what I call shoulders or network, they choose the easy way to climb the success and the ladder to the position they want which others deserve because they are more qualified for it, therefore the lazy gets up and the hard working fellow stays underground!.

When you rely on yourself and this is the best to do, you are mostly stuck, tired and frustrated, it is always good to have a handy-man, a friend that helps you in your difficult times... I never had one.

CHAPTER 8

I'm looking there, I see a tall damaged church, with high sharp pointed roof and towers, it got damaged and hit, some parts are destroyed completely, a big brown dirt separates us, the church is in the middle of nowhere, in my mind, what happened to this place? sad and abandoned!

Now, I see people getting a wish to be

realized, I'm not one of them, I'm OK for now, no need for anything.

I see, up a high level, an unfamiliar guy getting his wish to jump on the white horse to a dark unknown place, he will come back and will be returning to where he started, really?

It's a frightening height, but it's his wish, the white horse was a real stunning beauty, sirens are the ones asking each individual for wishes to be realized, one of them came to us "people", I didn't even answered, it's understood that I'm not doing it, I'm holding Lisa and was surprised when Sam said: "yes, I wish to meet with the shark deep in the waters", I'm asking Lisa to stay right where she is, to make sure Sam will return after diving the deepest with the siren, in my mind, I don't trust her to maintain her word and bring him back to the surface, I felt, she lied and she is covering something, a secret, I couldn't just trust her, I had no idea what's gonna happen down there? But Sam wanted to go, so be it, Lisa is holding me, not letting me go, I have to rush to catch up With them then follow them without her "siren" knowing, she doesn't have any right on me, to control me or anything like that, since I didn't express any wish to her, I'm free and not depending on her.

I see a very nice car, the front door has a group of keys in it, Kelly has a beautiful new white car, good for her! we are getting in it together, I asked her to drive us somewhere other then where we are.

In her office, somebody is mean, not professional, her supervisor is not a good guy nor a good worker, unqualified person to hold a supervisor's position, she deserves a better supervisor.

I went to report the injustice and bad treatment to the manager's secretary, she listened or pretended to do so, she didn't take any action, I'm like what is this work place, full of unqualified workers?

The issue was that the woman who was abusing and mistreating Kelly, her boss, she was mean, creating a lot of issues to Kelly, when I reported her, the secretary pointed to four more women supposed to be the mean woman's sisters and said that she cannot do anything to that woman because she has a family support that can create more issues, that support or person was a wealthy guy!.

The manager knew about what the ugly supervisor did to Kelly, he went to see him mentioning to him to never do it again, that he should stop being that bad, I saw him pointing at him while talking, but the supervisor is a mean nasty dark person, he doesn't have really any respect to the manager and treats him like nobody, in fact they are both bodies, they know each other very well!

The mean supervisor had a desk in the middle of the hall, near the coke machine, to get served whenever he wishes, to see all and every single thing moving and hear every detail! Isn't he mean?!.

I reported to Kelly everything, in my mind, the people there don't care about work, they are unqualified and unprofessional, lacking leadership,

hard work and even motivation.

Kelly knew all that, so I'm like let's go, get to the car and drive out of here!

I see the theater's stage, a group of young girls and boys training for the show, they have a performance, a competition one, they need to stand out if they wish to stay and get selected.

One particular girl did go over the top practicing and got hurt falling from the stairs.

Who in a million years, wants to acrobat over the stairs?! She just jumped without counting how many stairs left to be able to land on one, she misplanned the whole thing, she is recovering now, in a couple of days she will be just fine and ready to compete for her team.

It's a team's effort and work to survive and make the best performance out of it, they are dressed with shiny beautiful outfits, the boys too are working towards making it a good experience.

They have a dorm, sort of rooms to talk and visit each other.

Time to have my coffee with the toasted bread topped with butter! Yum...

I heard my father, he is calling me, kind of mentioning my name to go and see him, I'm rushing downstairs, there are too many of them, built almost in a circular way, the style of the 19th century, but before stepping down the last one I said: "dad! why did you call me?", he replied: "I didn't call you at all, I didn't ask you to come", in my mind, I didn't want him to call me down where he is, and the strange thing is that he was a big grey ostrich sitting at his desk, now I see his back, being busy he is asking me to go back, up, to where I was, I understood he had no interest in me being there, and that he wasn't to bother me at all because he is busy with his work...

I recall what previously happen when he called me and insisted, from that dark and frightening place, he knew I miss him, I went to see him then, I opened the metal gate and went to him even knowing it's a dangerous place to be in, I couldn't resist him calling me, I trusted him, but on my way, a dark force wanted to catch me, others that I don't know who they were, were trying to get out, the dark force approached, I knew it was dangerous and I was basically in a place for the dead, I was going to be one of them! I screamed: "why daddy did you call me? I trusted you never will harm me, but you tricked me to get me caught here forever, I don't want to stay here, I want to get back, up there...".

I, somehow, in a lightning speed jumped the stairs and locked the chain of the gate to not allow the force to get me, the lock wasn't going to hold for long, still I'm not safe, but I escaped for now, and that's what happened before I went downstairs to ask him the reason for him calling me again, but instead this time he didn't call me, it was my imagination hearing him mentioning my name, he was busy and interested in his work, he asked me to get upstairs, back to where I came from!.

CHAPTER 9

I'm walking, weird enough with Paul who passed away.

He is carrying his two luggage, it's too heavy for him I taught, so I took one from his hand, Nancy mentioned that I shouldn't because I'm sick and hurt, in my mind, I shouldn't lift heavy things, she is right, but couldn't help it and even suffering myself from the heavy lift, I did it, in the other hand I had my own luggage, but where are we heading to?

where are they? who are they? In my mind, it's like a journey, similar to going to a hotel room? Or, a hospital?.

We got there, we have been told that it's the room, I recall three beds, one for Nancy, Weird, on the side I showed Paul his bed to relax from the tiring lifting and walking, but what about the third bed? who is it for? Me...?

I need to go pee, I went all the way down to the other side for toilets, I was shy to do it in the ones near by people, on the way I see this guy looking at me from his office thinking that I'm a new face, new to the company, it's normal to be curious and look with interest, he is younger, with black tick and curly hair, I passed by his office, didn't say hi, he knew I'm there for the toilets because it's the end of the tall hall, I made the turn but the guy I was earlier talking to rushed and passed me and took it, he cheated me, in my mind, he followed me and knew exactly where I was going then did the same by steeling the idea to pee, I knocked on the other toilet, I'm in rush to do it, it was another guy there, he took a long time to pee, he should be done by now, I'm thinking it's my turn to do it, but guess what! he wouldn't get out and was trying for more just by holding the toilet for himself, no way to pee.

Now, I'm called and have to rush to the big room, it's the classroom but on the way and wearing a short school skirt I peed a tiny bit, cleaned it with my hand and did try to hold it thinking that it's embarrassing if I pee on myself, isn't it?.

The girl that called me took me to the classroom where a teacher that I knew somehow was holding a book and reading to all of us stating Mandarin is one of the hardest languages to learn, in my mind, I know this language, only I know it, I went close to her to get something, a pink box and other stuff that seemed mine, she asked me to hold on to them for a little while, I didn't mind, went and took a seat next to the girl who called me earlier, people painting their faces blue, not the guys, do the girls "we" found it high fashion and amazing to do? In the closets behind me girly dresses that me and the girl taught might be a good idea to try on once done with the lecture, there is a continuing hall on the left dark side of the classroom, where the girls go change and put makeup on as well as getting to the classroom directly.

I'm at the train station waiting, me and the girl that I ignore the name "the teacher" is like: "you take the coming one, sit here, is it comfortable or not for you she asked?" I replied, it's fine, I'm not cold just waiting for my train to take me where I should be...

It all began with me walking, and on my way I knew a face of a guy I met before, somewhere, must be at work, he said hi and I replied, in my mind I didn't want to meet any previous known face, he asked me about jobs and I wished him good, he mentioned that the manager will hire soon and is looking for some people, in my mind,

I might be one of them, the manager seemed nice... Since when? I don't think he ever liked me! Anyway, we all stood in the big patio listening to his speech, in my mind, the guy I met is trying to impress him to be picked, I went out looking for the toilets, didn't want to use the ones close by but the guy was watching me and followed me instead and took in no time the toilet I wanted! in my mind, I'm gonna comeback and hopefully one of the two toilets is empty to pee!

I don't feel right, I'm tired, in pain, my stomach! From the coffee perhaps? I'm lazy, dizzy, am I having a cold? I wonder? I took the luggage from Paul to help, I should've not done it, I'm sick, I cannot hold the day, I tried to get some rest, what's happening to me? I'm not myself, I'm locked in kind of a game show, who wins gets out.

kids are held there behind a big door, for depot! Every time a parent or a family friend wins the kids are released, the one they came to play for in the first place, I'm talking to the host, she seems nice explaining the rules, he, that guy I don't know him got the book, he pushed it on the table, it went to the other side of the wall and voila one kid got released, I couldn't see the faces just the feet, I mean the shoes and sandals, who are they? why are they locked!?

All what I know is that the game has to keep going to free more kids.

I see an old ceramic fountain, the people passing by, in my mind let's have some water, after all it's good to have some water in case thirsty, a family, parents, friends and kids, that girl had a headband, wearing a white dress is it a special occasion? they are "the people" heading to...? I don't know? The next thing is that they want that specific guy, Sam, and after all their attempts, they sent this big breast, big bum young girl, for it, that was the game in its way of ending, I didn't agree to do that, we didn't know, it was a surprise! I'm sure he will be pleased with it, she is planning to do everything to get him having sex with her, after all she is an expert and he will fall definitely for it, in my car the driver is driving, I see a cliff and a fast river, deep down the white color of the fast stream stood out so clearly that I remember it.

She sits on me, she is big and talking to my

driver about her plans, he, the driver seems to like her already, she seduced him, fast! She shows him one breast, he is impressed loving it, then showed him her bums, she is so sure of herself she moved forward showing me how good she is in seducing rubbing her bums against mine it feels tempting and good, in my mind I need to have se...

That's not good, It's the afternoon, prepared some bread and coffee for myself, did I really had that "sex", it hurts like hell, this is not the first time...

It all began, me in the yard, sort of a park, it's sunny and I own kind of a small "wind mill" play, the girl approached me and asked if her family, the boy can use it, I said yes, for the kids only but not for others, she puts the boy he is having fun, I moved away, I see this little girl the daughter of a nasty and mean man, it's bad to see him, I mentioned to him that I wanted to hold her, he didn't seem to trust me but then watching me holding her, the way I promised to take care of her, the way I looked at him saying I didn't see her for at least a year at that moment he let's go of his daughter's hand trusting me to be with her, is his daughter that much grown up? since when? She was a year and half, I remember her diaper she was wearing it in a very bright room, her name was Amy...

It all started with her, then moved to the game show then to the sex temptation of that big breasted woman trying to seduce someone she and all wanted to destroy his life to prove he is not worth the trust.

The bread machine is so noisy, I wonder if it's broken? In my mind, why did I make bread? Why?.

CHAPTER 10

She, my friend Kelly is trying to marry the supposed to be king, Zoe is trying to get her and help her to do so, after I didn't show any interest in marrying him, in my mind, Nancy! how could you and all even suggest me such a thing? I met the guy, but he is not a king, he's Mel, he seems ill after his wife was gone, I said to him hi and bye, hope you recover, try to get some rest, that's all the conversation with him, I didn't do what was supposed to be done, get him to like me and think I'm the one, but instead Kelly went to him and made him laugh and showed him how much she cares for him, and Mel liked it, I think he prefers her, and even his witch mom prefers her than me, why? Is she jealous of me? does she hates me to the point where she prefers another girl with her son instead of me?

Anyway, Zoe helping Kelly and opening the secret box to teach her the game of making him attracted to her, Zoe is good when it comes to advises and wisdom.

I saw him again, but he is ill, he has kids I said to Kelly, she replied: "and so what?" In my mind she accepted the fact and was willing to do anything to go and live with him! A shocker it's all about money and about location.

I see him in a chair, this time he is nicer to me, does he like me? Deep inside, I don't want him to do so!.

The witch, Mel's mother, controls her son, whatever she orders him to do he does, he is her puppet, who wants to be with a such week puppet? I see him by the stairwell standing there,but, in my mind, he has to lie down on the bed, in that not so bright room.

I'm in a kind of desert, that portion is for cobras, I should be careful, there is a house full of people it's like a hospital but for care, snakes everywhere, we know and are fine with it.

It's so sunny but yet dangerous, I'm upstairs, on the other level, I can handle them, but a cobra is fast, I need to get inside and quick, right now they are asleep, but not all, few are watching still, I'm in this box that has tiny black and white bunnies from Australia, "they are unique and not found anywhere else", the person was telling me, I held one and it stopped moving! did I hurt it without knowing while busy in my previous conversation? I put it down with the others and watched... it started to move again changing it's color to white, I'm telling Tyra to be gentle with them, they are very rare and sensitive!

In my mind, let's get out of here, lets go! Cactus, desert, sand and heat with snakes... Let's change the scene.

I got the notice from the lead, he is happy I'm not! Why me? in my mind, it is not fair and is unjust, anyway I have to get out, get my stuff of many years out of the office fast, because they want it empty in no time.

I'm waiting for the elevator, I see Daniel with his sexy shirt, he is famous and terribly handsome, he is waiting for me but I turned my back like I wasn't there for the elevator, in my mind, he is too attractive to be with him in that small space, I heard that no woman resists him.

I'm with the lead after he heard me saying that they aren't nice, that they are in fact unjust, he came to me, asking me to repeat what he heard from my mouth loudly to a group of nasty people, I denied each word because I want to get a job somewhere else and I know they can destroy my chances to get one, he is holding my hand and kissed it, he pretends to be very sad and sorry for what he has done, I don't believe him but still played the game, he wants to kiss a goodbye, no way in my mind! so all what I come up with is to tell him that we might kiss lips accidentally and I don't want that to happen, he shook his head of agreement.

I see that girl, she is not a nice one, the office building is like in a deserted field full of snakes and too hot, I want out and fast, I went to the bus stop and asked for the desert one, it was almost a day trip to head down where my stuff are, I didn't have to pee! It was relaxing, long but relaxing and easy trip, I'm looking for my shirts and my glasses? Where are they? I need to find them!.

I'm looking for a toilet to pee, I wanted out, I need to, most of them "toilets" are piled of poop or full of pee, I don't want my shoes "soft material" to get wet, I'm trying for one, it is so slow.

Oh! The opening windows are low enough to see me peeing, why didn't I check it before, are they able to see my naked bottom? I'm starting to worry, then my head is like who cares move on being that uptight, I'm still collecting my stuff from different toilets, the whole place is sectioned to toilets and halls, weird place to be in, the sun is hitting the place, I need to get out and enjoy.

I noticed that one of the windows belongs to a dangerous creature that can harm humankind, I need to hide and take the right way to head back to town, am I empty enough to take a long bus trip back? I'm not sure, I need to make a decision and quick, the woman approached me and yelled at me because I was inside her place, her work space, she is angry I'm there what's her business with me? Why is she that uptight and mean to me? she yells and I jumped from being that loud yelled at, I desire the plates of grapes and other fruits, she is looking after, I'm hungry but couldn't touch any just contemplated the whole feast without touching or taking, that's so bad! I head towards the bus station, I'm at the town, few blocks from home, I need another bus, in my mind, let's have a walk after all it saves me money not to pay a bus ticket, it's getting very dark, I can barely see the roads, the people, and everything else, I am almost there...?.

Everybody knew about how bad the boss of that company was, he hired a killer that cuts peoples bodies and slaughtered them too, bodies are hanged by the feet full of blood everywhere on high strings, he is looking to finish the rest of us, I saw his face, I'm running, everybody is away from him.

All what happened to began with is us knowing that the policy of the company, the rules and standards are false and introduced just to blind us "people", and get us away from the real ugliness of those in charge of it, it's disgusting.

I see the killer, I'm behind the wall I'm watching and heard every word of the boss who hired him.

Suddenly, I'm with Kim, she is sitting on the chair getting ready for the show, I opened the drawer and picked a bottle of perfume, an expensive one, to spray some on her, perfume is a good luck, then another girl did the same, Kim mentioned that we should stop that, because she put already enough, she is cute and down to earth, I can still recall her beautiful black, soft hair, wavy and shiny, she was wearing a beautiful dress that enhances her curves.

Now, I'm talking to her at the desk, hers apparently, it's like I work for her to get her ready for shows and things like that, we are facing a huge window that looks at the whole city, what a beautiful scene, and the light is coming strong to enlighten the office or room we are in, I'm saying to her that the most important thing to her right now is her beautiful daughter, she agrees, in my mind she has a boy, a son as well, she got pregnant and had a brother to her gorgeous little girl.

I can feel her happiness with her husband, she has respect for him, for herself and too much love for the family, again she gives me the feeling of a normal girl that knows her assets but yet still listen and walk on the ground.

CHAPTER 11

I landed a simple job in the old company, the one they kicked me out of it, in my mind, is it the only place to get a job from? I hated it, I was discriminated and treated like trash, I was always the one that cleans the mess of others and worse the one that does their jobs get paid less while they get promotions and hundreds of thousands "salary and bonuses", what a mess that place was, if you know someone holding a high position, you get to pee on the rest like myself, the boss is giving me his political "fake" nice face, the one you trust right away thinking it must somehow somewhere some descent people left in this world, well guess what? None is left, this kind has been exterminated by his "the boss" kind, full of corruption and doing favors to his close friends and to those he drinks with and eats with, his close surrounding poisoned his ears with crap.

I see that piece of sesame bread, not big, still I want it so badly, I'm looking at it like if it was in a big full of light shopping window flying in the air and staring at me and me at it, I mentioned how much that piece was better than the one I'm doing right now because that's what I wanted, anyway the job I went back to was ending, quickly... I need to find something else, in my mind, not bad! I made some money that will keep me running and paying my bills for sometime.

I'm sitting on the floor, my legs are joined to hold red hood and poncho like coat for her, "Tina", to protect her from the bad weather and the wind, I see this on her to be a real nice coat, I look at her, in my mind, the wind is so strong!.

I'm rushing, I need to pee now, in front of me an old woman, I said: "sorry, I'm first and I really need to go", she agrees as she didn't start running until she saw me and heard my need then she wanted to do it.

I closed the door, but it's made of glass, she can see and hear everything, from the toilet I'm like: "please you are not supposed to look", I looked and her head, weird enough, was big inside and through the glass door, she answered that she agrees and that she is looking at the wall away, I then needed some paper to clean, it's all gone so I had to cut some cotton from the inside of my long dress to use instead, I'm looking at the garbage and people in my mind do so weird things, the poop is on the top of the garbage big can, in my mind, that person whoever needed badly to go so used it as a toilet, after all there is only one available and people had to take turns to use it, I threw the piece of cotton than found myself somewhere else talking to Nancy, she is mentioning how sad and upset she is for what happened to Oliver, she prefers to take care of him making sure he will be fine instead of coming and visiting me, she was turning the big square pool's fresh water with the cooking spoon and talking about her interest and worries, I do understand, in my mind why is she mentioning all that!.

I'm working hard, got all the paper asked from me ready for the boss, I'm happy doing my job, someone came over asking for some documents while trying to find them for her, my boss called me and in front of her was treating me like garbage, without any respect, she, who is a total real Trash, I wasn't bothered at all, I guess because it's not my job after all.

The Trash was staring with shock at him but at the same time giving me orders and bad remarks, I guess watching him treating me like shit, she did the same.

I knew then that I shouldn't be her assistant.

I'm going downstairs, with my sort of boyfriend, both we ended at a tiny cage that yet had thousands of military guys trapped in there, I was ordered to go and check on them to make sure they are OK, but all of them started coming to me complaining about their wish to be set free, they didn't like it there at all, the commander seemed like a nice guy getting along with everybody, I wasn't happy for them to be where they are, the cage was the size of a doll's house and only I had the keys to open the big cage like a jail's door, suddenly, I hear laughs, people making fun of me treating me as a stupid person, telling me that whatever I do is not smart, any job I undertake I'm not capable of assuming my responsibilities, in my mind I'm embarrassed, you could hear their laughs, why are they mean to me? Treating me like garbage and in fact a big barrel was there in the center of us, the group standing around it.

I'm holding something in my hands, wearing black gloves, my head down, I still hear them making jokes and insulting me with all kind of mean words, I looked up and I'm kissing the guy with big black hair, it's like I like him and I want more but he doesn't want to kiss me.

I climbed with my body up the yellow wall

where he is glued to ask him for another kiss, got just a slight lips touch and went back down on the bed, behind the wall I hear voices and people stating things regarding me getting the job or not, people I knew and met before in the last work's place, they are happy and trying to get all for just themselves not sharing an inch with me, in the past I helped these people to be where they are today, but we all know if you do good bad will be returned to you, it's just the way it works with this type of people.

I wonder if they belong to the human category!.

I have a huge headache, thinking, my coffee is first to have with an omelette which I made to enjoy the day.

CHAPTER 12

I'm in a big room, like a library or something similar, group of women there arguing about who is right? A man, nasty malicious is there I don't trust him, he is there to harm me specially why? It's like he knows the three women, the room is semi-dark with huge open windows that looks out to the hall of an old 1800 building, lots of traffic of people passing through the hall, I hear noise and conversations all the way, I look through the window to check it out and the mean guy comes to me advising me this and that, in my mind just don't upset him but also don't get too friendly pretend to listen and try to find your way out of this place.

Finally, I escaped the place and ran, I meet downstairs on my way out of the mall the three women, I first saw the shirts hanging at the wall, specially the Chinese style one, looks fancy but was on sale, I don't know if it will fit me, still I want it no matter which size it is, it's cheap and attractive and reminds me of my old one that I gave away, I'm touching it, suddenly another hand came to pick it, I taught for a second I lost it but it sticked to my hand and the girl couldn't get it and not only this I picked two more shirts of a unique style as well, they envy my choice, they want all the three styles I've picked, in my mind no way I'm taking those three, one girl seems like working in the store came over to me stating that the size will not fit me because it's in between small and medium, in my mind I'll manage to fit in no problem, I tried it on, I'm so bothered by these three women, cleaning all the dust out of a low counter, cleaning kind of the place for the supervisor to find it neat, she stretched her arm on my hand to reach for the dust, I didn't care to help, after all I'm here to pick the three shirts.

I'm on a very high bridge, looking down, at far sight is the mall where I was? I'm out without paying, I got all three shirts for free, in my mind, I better go back and pay for them, what if this and that?.

I don't want any trouble caused by a genuine mistake, me... forgetting to pay, them... not charging me a cent, and the alarm... not making a sound to remind me!.

Usually tracking or alarm tags are attached to the items you buy but not those three as they were on sale, perhaps? I want to go back and pay for them, but they were so cheap why to bother, I want to be honest with myself but why look stupid and go back, what's the point, what's the purpose, and what am I trying to prove to people I don't even know?.

I see the mall's security guy doing his job with professionalism, I'm on the very high "near to the sky" bridge far away, and here I'm trying to go back just to be honest not stealing anything and pay for what I got! Suddenly, I'm trying to find the way inside, going up and down the stairs, that mean guy again, I don't want to be his friend, I sat on a stair, similar to the theater's stairs for watching a movie, I went again upstairs, that was the last level no more, I'm trying to be discreet and not talk to anyone, I'm sitting on a theater's stair, I hear Zoe enjoying her boat trip with her new boyfriend, his accent is from a village, very heavy, he is tall, but she was happy, she went on the boat that came back like a speed of light from a tropical warm place, reminded me of Italy's boat trip I've taken once, I'm trying not to be seen by her, after all it doesn't matter if I say hi or not she is busy and good for her to have some fun.

I'm sitting beside who is supposed to be my supervisor, she, the trash charmed him again, he likes the type that flirts with everyone, she is married but boy she is after everyone, he presented his condolence to her taking advantage of the situation to show her his affection, trash... She always charms my supervisors, he has a beard and mine is longer and blond color, I'm touching it stating in my mind how long it is, same as a ponytail, soft and shiny, I looked to my left, my friend Rachel is doing her bed, she is undusting it getting it ready and prepared for the night, she undusted her blanket and tapped the twin mattress, she is certainly busy.

I see my friend Kelly she is at the back of the big room, the office, the supervisor called, this time she replied from her seat, didn't want to get close to him, he wants her in front of him to watch her actions closely. She knows his plan and preferred not to move, and that's for the best, he has bad intentions and thoughts, he is mean by nature.

I'm outside, I see Kelly heading towards a path, a hidden one! I'm worried about her safety, I have to move fast and guide her.

The so called trash is watching me wanting to copy as always each inch act I do, I escaped and made it to the path, now I'm in a whole new tunnel for cars to pass through, in my mind finally they built the road to make an easy traffic, but is it safe? No safety precautions were taken, they relied on the sun's day light, but what about the night's traffic? I looked at the mountains, on both sides of the road, is that good enough for protection? I don't think so...

I'm in a school, a private fancy one from the look, for the opening day, few kids were brought by their parents to run a level test, there is a long buffet for everyone, behind the counter a girl and a boy watching who needs what to serve the guests, the parents, I wanted so badly a desert, so I went and grabbed some myself but then went back again to get two pieces of the chocolate ones, the girl looked at me unhappy, it's like I shouldn't do this and should just grab one and that's all, I didn't care I wanted them and I got them, now in the open room with that administration responsible for the papers of the school, she asked me to write my full name, I wondered and she answered that's the rule!

Is she an alien in a human appearance, came to gather information about me and him... Bob? I had to write it in an upside down way, suddenly I looked at Bob's face coming off, scared and panicking the old man explained the impact of the flu that "Bob" got, it's a nasty one!

I don't really want to put the details, but, I found myself in a 1800's soldier outfit, shot a gun fire at someone next to me in the carriage, jumped in the air then stood easily in front of the fancy expensive hotel where a huge flagpole was hooked tall! Looked, through one room I saw Nancy, I went in and was asked to iron a white with lace bride's outfit like, a sexy one piece satin bride's underwear, for Kelly! Why? simply because I spelled coffee on her outfit and had to do something nice that she forgives me.

Anyway that white outfit, I wanted it for me!.

I'm walking, watching the fancy houses holding Thor in my arms, suddenly, I turned and saw this black cab stopping in front of one of the buildings, it's her the witch, she is..., in my mind since when she wears black shiny leather outfits with lots of zippers, that's my style not hers! I looked at my outfit I'm wearing it, but, not all of it, I got the high thin boots, the pants, the sleeves..., I'm walking, she caught me passing by, oh no! I stole her outfit just for a tour after all it suits me better, and should be mine, I didn't want her to see Thor but she knew I'm holding someone, and at the crossing road her friends were there, they must've told her what I'm thinking... Anyway I apologized twice, in my mind I had to, but did I? She is a mean witch that harmed many people many times, is she back to hunt? She loves harming people and destroying them, she should be busy with her own life.

I didn't take of the outfit, it's mine!.

CHAPTER 13

I see Kelly sleeping on a mattress in the other room, the hall is so wide, I'm in a different one, she gets up fast and stood up in front of me, she broke a glass bottle, the ships are on the floor, some of them sticking to my white clean socks, I'm trying to smoothly get rid of them rubbing my feet against each other in a very careful way, I asked her why she's done it? she replied that it's OK to do so as she sometimes cries glass ship tears, so I looked deep in her eyes they were red she's done it before and it's OK in my mind, she is suddenly holding a big large kitchen knife it's so shiny mentioning she can cut the pieces of the broken bottle even smaller than they are.

I'm in a large room, this guy standing in front of me is dead, he is talking about his room's decoration, I asked him why he has the wind mill "wood" furniture? He replied that it's his room, that he is free to decorate it the way he wishes, he is free and I agreed, so I stopped asking about his room's decoration.

I see Paul, on a white bed, but what is strange is that he is having sex with another woman, other than his girlfriend, he is a cheater in my mind, she is out by the door waiting for him, it's sunny and bright where she is but he kept just doing what he wants, then met her later and lied to her again. As usual, in my mind, he cheated many times, and she thinks he is in love with her.

Why did I see such a thing? I like Paul, he is a nice person indeed.

I'm with Nancy, and I see that woman, a very mean one that keeps always harming people, she is the trash asking for bread, Nancy replied that there is none, I went to the kitchen and brought whatsoever was left, in my mind the family doesn't have enough food to eat, that homemade bread won't last long, but, still I went and wanted to hand it to the trash before I do I stopped to think about it one more time.

I'm in a big flat white land, nothing there, no plants no animals except for that guy looking serious, I'm afraid that he sees me, why? In my mind I shouldn't be seen by him, it's like someone frightening, he is not moving and looking straight in front of him, there is nothing facing him, I hope he doesn't turn towards me, I've had the feeling if that happens something extremely harmful will happen to me...

I see the sand mountains, I have to get there and out of here, I have to get to the other side where I can meet human being, someone..., here I see the endless white land and the high sky, I run towards the mountain, I'm climbing, in my mind I can do this no problem, behind me suddenly I hear a woman yelling at her I believe son: "look she is doing it we can do it too just keep climbing son", I'm almost to the top it's getting slippery with all the sand, will I make it to the top? All what I'm doing is trying to grab the sand with my nails to be able to climb and get to the other world!

I'm sitting with my friend Kelly, she is talking to her new hot friend, in my mind mmmm... she knows as usual who to pick as a friend and she always knew, I like him, he seems like a nice guy, genuine and smart, I'm thirsty and he holds a plastic bottle of water that he bought, he didn't mind to give it to me and to drink from, he didn't mind that's unusual, but now the bottle is dripping the water on my head, it's open from the bottom, I'm getting water but on my head and face, we all, the three of us are seriously talking, is it a war? what is it? I see in the room very serious people talking to each other.

I'm going to slide on that scary mountain, got out of the car and I'm helping the friend of Kelly "Noah" showing him the rules of sliding up, it takes just effort to know, practice some tips and techniques that's all, then it's very easy to do it! Why do I want to climb up again?.

The two policemen came to check that I'm OK, because that place drops a lot of people not supposed to be there, it's like this is so special kind of a mountain and you need permission to be there, the guy "Noah" is with me I mentioned to them, they took it easy then and helped with the equipment.

They helped us to get started, I'm training Noah to stand still on the surfing flat surface.

I'm looking at the sky now in a huge field looks like, the sky is higher than usual, suddenly the guy in the pulley truck dropped a heavy rectangular metal shaped box that has a glass window inside it I could see the thermos, I'm thinking, in my mind must be some sort of a liquid milk in it!? Puzzled I'm walking trying to get out of this mess, Zoe is with me, I'm advising her to be very careful and look always where she puts her feet because things from these machines might fall anytime and crush people without notice, in my mind a big construction is going on here, and huge pulleys are used for the purpose.

I see Zoe chained to the wall, lying on the floor of the room trying to tell me something about a friend, a cheater, she is with me and taking my side, her left hand cuffed and chained, the black chain is keeping her down on the side of her body, we are talking about our old home, used to be attached to my middle school which from its door I could go right to my apartment in couple minutes.

It was the good time I was teenager again, in my mind and going back to the time where I'm heading through the teacher's access door right to the big hall of my building where my apartment is at the first level, in my mind, I'm living the event again, the principle of the school allows me to use the special door.

I see Kelly, she is mean this time, why did she rent the apartment next to me to him Sam! Without telling, me what's her plan? I wonder? She is using Rachel as an excuse to her reasons for choosing this particular apartment, all what happened is that she came for a visit, there are constructions going on outside, but other than that my area seemed equipped with the stores you need to get your groceries from in no time, and without even driving your car, but, is that a good reason for her to rent this apartment? I didn't think so, I'm listening to her conversation with Rachel, to who I said hi, I heard Kelly talking to the building manager stating that yes she's gonna take the place to live in, but really it was Rachel's new place, she had a bed and few covers in her hands to use. Rachel is putting down her luggage to get ready to sleep and get some rest, I went to speak to Kelly asking her to get away from my place but in vain, seemed like her and Sam are planning something because he doesn't mind, it's like he expected it to happen and wanted it to, in my mind I'm strangling him to quit the plan and tell me the truth behind Kelly moving close, but he kept smiling and my fingers were slipping out even trying hard to stick my nails in his skin.

The day before, I'm ironing my shirt because I have an appointment, a work interview, in my mind I have to look descent to get accepted, I see an insect crawling on the dusty floor's carpet, I asked Kelly to kill it and step on it with her black flat boots and she's done it, but I had to make sure it is killed, I didn't like that brown insect with black eyes. I'm with Nelly she is in the toilet, both feet up on each side of the wall to allow me to use the toilet, she is asking me to be careful about something? No idea what it is, I wanted to harm her and hit her, but she was OK, if I hurt her it's my safety or should I say I'm in trouble!.

In my mind, I'm holding a dead body wrapped in a black bed's sheet, walking on the right side of Sam to who I gave a baby to hold as to help me get out of the restaurant, a guy with the chef's hat is waiting for me there to get the body, suddenly the body moved and didn't stop moving, I unwrapped it fast to let some air in, who was he? I couldn't see, the guy on the sidewalk saw the whole scene and knew nobody will be given to him...not today!.

It's sunny, a beautiful blue sky up there, I'll enjoy the rest of my day.

They called, she is ill, very ill, a warning siren went on to evacuate the place and Tina had to go out in that freezing weather, no jacket no nothing to cover herself, she started vomiting without notice, her pains started to grow sharply, she had to get back home, her condition just got worse and worse...

Before getting to sign the ribbon, I'm looking for a land, a new one to grow and live, I could see still that place where kids live smart and happy, they built all the rockets there, so parents started to move out there to raise their kids, I heard so much about it that I went to check it myself, but up the mountain the bird is telling me to be careful and make sure that the black leopard doesn't see me, I'm trying to go back, I knew then that it's not the place I'm looking for to take people with me to.

That black thing went higher and didn't see me but at my big shock, just meters from my back was another nasty one who means to kill and harm, I'm like having a reddish cat or is it really a cat? Not a ...? I'm running away screaming to my two friends to do the same, to run, one locked herself in the car, I can still hear the sound of the locks, one was inside a building with a solid door, but me... I was out still running away, he captured the poor little red cat but I see in front of it a grey-white one! He got the young cat I said, I hear the cracked bones it's terrifying, I had time to be safe, and no harm was done to me... But who was the little cat? That frightens me? in my mind never I'll take people to that place which sounded like frightening... Isn't it? That's where I'm planning to go to... Not anymore!

I'm in sort of a challenge where I have to sign my name on ribbons, I helped design a new hair band and the marketer will help advertise for it, so she asked me to sign the twenty ribbons, but I had to wait for some decorations first to be done before starting, there is this unknown girl, she is everywhere I go, she pretends to be my friend but is she really?.

In the car, out of it, in the show room, she is everywhere!, she heard the name I'm using for the show, I turned suddenly and here she is listening as usual pretending it's a pure coincidence, I walked away heading towards the kitchen but in the entrance here is Eric lying down in a basin full of water, in my mind what is he doing here other than making my way to the place difficult, I made it though, got what I wanted and headed to the car waiting for me, we stopped at an indoor roller coaster's park, I was asked to hold Abby but I dropped her badly on the front body, the floor was hard and bitumen, again I'm frightened what's going on? Next, I hear her laughing with David, she got to sit in her favorite carousel, very well decorated, I asked and yelled that she gets out of it, she couldn't hear me, too noisy there, I'm looking at the weird place, and headed to a yellow room's Theater, there is a plastic hammer and that black haired boy following my steps, I don't like him nor trust him.

I'm out of the indoor playground, I looked up, it's dark but I could see the ferris wheel getting high up and out of the place from an opening whole in the roof, in my mind that was really fun then, not boring at all, I'm on the couch, a dark faced person in Zoe's face is telling me about her high school skills, in my mind that was somebody else good at school not her, and anyway who is that guy pretending to be her "Zoe"? The face had a fuggy dark fume like color.

I see her, Joanne, getting me ready, dressed me with my bridle white dress and sent me to a big room where a high ranked priest is, in my mind I shouldn't be allowed to be there, but because the long tail of my dress was tight with blue ribbons I passed the competition and was allowed to model in a silent ambiance, Joanne didn't enter and stopped right at the entrance, in my mind I'm too old to be there, my hair is messed up and my skin is not soft enough, but I put down the veil that covered me and made me pass for a younger bride modeling in front of the priests.

I'm having my coffee now, as usual, I was still thinking, am I dy...?.

CHAPTER 14

Nancy is making flat bread, a huge quantity and a huge size, I want one, I'm waiting for the lunch time, she called us to sit as usual around the silver big plate, I see people around having more than one piece, everybody started eating, Nancy didn't put any for me, I'm not happy, in fact I'm so angry at her, as usual she has that scarf covering like a turbine her hair, she looks younger and stronger, I let her know about my disagreement with the way she gave the pizza and left me with none, I did swear she is coming to hit me, I'm down on the floor incapable to stand and defend myself, she is coming closer to harm me, in my mind she hit me than took me by the neck and strangled me, I'm suffocating, I'm trying to get out of her hands but in vain, I'm screaming loud, my throat hurts, it is in pain and very sore, so I grabbed a cup of water to clear it up.

They are calling for her "Brenda", the guy came to check on her, I'm sick worried she has a high fever, she couldn't sleep properly and kept flipping back and forth turning and kicking, she is very uncomfortable with that fever rising, talking through all the night in her sleep, I run to bring the blanket to cover her from the cold, I looked through the half door half window I see her dressed in yellow, I stayed outside watching, the place was crowded with kids running all over the big room, I went, got my coffee and headed back to watch a movie.

I'm on a huge boat, at first I was exploring the many parts of it, it looked just like a yellow building, I was talking to Nelly about things, then decided to go to meet someone, I'm on the covered deck, kind of a long hall and I'm looking at the big metal seems to me the fluorescent light, no light was on, it was just a decoration thing, in my mind that thing can create a lot of safety issues, I didn't finish my thought and the heavy ball fell down, the boat lost balance, soon no surface, it's starting to sink, I jumped the stairs down towards Nancy and others Tania and Brenda, I have to get them and quick out of here, the dock is getting higher, so no one can climb to the ground, my father is alerting us and asking me to save them, the rocking ball is taking us down and even though in my mind if I save them I will not have a chance to save myself, I'm heavily breathing, thinking I'm sinking to the deep!

It's him Joe, I met him when I was 18 years old at the camping summer beach, it's a family camp, and you have to be accompanied by adults and family to make it inside, even visitors need a name or a reference to be allowed to get in the camp.

I'm with him, holding him, we are kissing, weird kisses, in my mind, he is not as cute as I thought, he is wearing a brown expensive jacket with a white wool collar, he is taller than me, but still we seem like very much in love, we are standing at the court of the university, we are young, and strong, then suddenly I'm in a hall, a dark one, I see some light coming from a barber room, I didn't care for it I kept walking but Joe's hand caught me and dragged me inside where he is sitting on a chair waiting for a man, I'm in love with him, in my mind what if Nancy saw me? She, will make a big deal, I have to hide him! But she found his jacket in the room of our house, I'm hurrying to tell him, and here he is coming out of the bath, his chest is shiny and has some black hair on, he quickly, seeing Nancy coming puts a towel on him to cover himself, everything went smooth and he was welcomed home to stay and eat.

<u>CONCLUSION</u>

I couldn't understand the surroundings and why things happened to me the way they did or still do? Found that the world we live in can be a mix of emotions, stress and depression, but, I try to forget and I try to forgive which is not easy, the events are the way my mind sees them and the thoughts that go through my head then, some parts of life are made by us, some by others that can be nice but mostly that can be harsh, and the way we deal with issues reflects our daily life!. Doesn't it?!.